THE
VANISHING
ACT

(& The Miracle After)

ESSENTIAL POETS SERIES 303

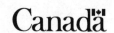

ONTARIO ARTS COUNCIL
CONSEIL DES ARTS DE L'ONTARIO

an Ontario government agency
un organisme du gouvernement de l'Ontario

Canada Council   Conseil des arts
for the Arts   du Canada

Guernica Editions Inc. acknowledges the support of
the Canada Council for the Arts and the Ontario Arts Council.
The Ontario Arts Council is an agency of the Government of Ontario.

We acknowledge the financial support of the Government of Canada

Mirabel

THE VANISHING ACT

(& The Miracle After)

GUERNICA
EDITIONS

TORONTO • CHICAGO • BUFFALO • LANCASTER (U.K.)
2023

Guernica Founder: Antonio D'Alfonso

Michael Mirolla, general editor
Anna van Valkenburg, editor
Cover and interior design: Rafael Chimicatti
Cover image: Caique Nascimento, Unsplash
Guernica Editions Inc.
287 Templemead Drive, Hamilton, (ON), Canada L8W 2W4
2250 Military Road, Tonawanda, N.Y. 14150-6000 U.S.A.
www.guernicaeditions.com

Distributors:
University of Toronto Press Distribution (UTP)
5201 Dufferin Street, Toronto (ON), Canada M3H 5T8
Independent Publishers Group (IPG)
814 N Franklin Street, Chicago, IL 60610, U.S.A
Gazelle Book Services, White Cross Mills
High Town, Lancaster LA1 4XS U.K.

First edition.
Printed in Canada.

Legal Deposit – First Quarter
Library and Archives Canada Cataloguing in Publication

Title: The vanishing act (& the miracle after) / Avleen Mokha (Mirabel).
Names: Mokha, Avleen, author.
Series: Essential poets ; 303.
Description: Series statement: Essential poets series ; 303 | Poems.
Identifiers: Canadiana 20230150764 | ISBN 9781771837958 (softcover)
Classification: LCC PS8626.O448625 V36 2023 | DDC C811/.6—dc23

CONTENTS

The Vanishing Act

(& The Miracle After)

The Vanishing Act

IDEATION

The idea came to me
like a word is whispered
in a vacant room.

A new opening, a spare
set of keys. Greet the neighbours
but don't let them peek.

You've got a green thumb
so leaf through my pages.
Here we never say what we mean
in the rare event
that we hear ourselves.

Instead, we speak from a distance
but I can't hear you
till you are on the floor,
and I am on the floor,
and the glass half full
has been turned upside down.

I shut the blinds, close shop,
stop answering calls. Forgiveness
is amorphous till you know
who it's for. Patience is a bargain
with a barbaric god. Disinvoke
your memory of me. I'm leaving
to be a version of me
that only I can see.

DIFFUSING TENSIONS

In therapy, a woman teaches
a woman how to make peace
with terror. How to sit cross-
hearted with four-day-old
hope. To see the ashes of
her childhood as fertility, not as
failure. Her brain awash with mindfulness,
she is to be, peacefully,
tranquilized.

The knot, appeased, reveals itself:
Nothing is criminal unless it harms a man.

What of the anger, so logical,
ingrained in the woman's head.
What of the fury of a nine-year-old
girl, raging and divisive.

Anger is not a weapon
in these feminine hands.
A trace of litigious violence.
Merely a childish threat of detonation.

HANDLE WITH CARE

It is the breakability of things
which allows them to be beautiful. There are

tragedies you wish you could have avoided. This
is what makes them tragic. I sing

of impossible worlds, where soft stays
soft. Where love stays love. You try to

tell me that, in our world, some things that we love
might break. The ground beneath me has left

to hold more stable legs. My mouth
has become glass under your gaze.

You can break me with your breath. I am so
delicate in this world that keeps on breaking.

It is the kind of beauty I wish did not exist.

NIGHTLIFE

In Wuhan, I saw men flocking
like damp pigeons after rain
to pop champagne. It reminded me
to take my coffee with spite.

In an alternate world, I would leave
your pulse. Take off the ring, choose
a different engagement. Write down religious differences.
Leave court early to prime my lids,
to pat on pressed pigments. Drain my tears
down the sink, convert my evenings
to worship the nightlife.

On Saint-Laurent, men walk me to jazzed bars.
I always make sure to stay the extra time:
Walk to their revved-up cars, but refuse
to get inside. Then I head north:
numb toes, keys clutched.

University students still believe that littering
is a myth. The women with lips I'd rather kiss
are scrambling to find arms to hide behind.

The deli sells out. The shoe store closed
from grief. The Italian grocers are dead,
but we the living want to know
what still lies in store. Walking alone, I spy
a hobo jangling a coffee chain cup.

I've grown up enough to say no. But when I head towards the bus
pockets heavy with change, something catches up to me.

The perennial chill of a question never asked.
The seasonal disappointment of early withdrawal.

I am a wound with legs.
A book with words you've never heard.
In another world, you could have offered the touch of a glove.
You could have read my face, again and again,
and understood why talking of love brings me pain.

ILLEGIBLE

Bedroom floor lore says that long ago
they spoke, but never learned to read.
Uncombed, they sat squat on trains.
Dead already by mistake. In Delhi,

I heard a woman scream for the beating
engine in us. In Montreal, I heard a man lose
his eyes on a walk to the park:

Dogged, minds shorn of all hope,
they live out their lives mechanically.

The myth of disbelief sometimes
catches up to me. At least
they got, the illiterate lot,
a train for their dead-not-yet.

They give their bodies unprompted
to an illegible ache and pacify
the feeling that only takes.

All concurred that the murders occurred,
but no one was there
to write it down.

SEMBLANCE OF A NARRATIVE

(i)

some summers ago, my head floats
under sparkling water, nose blocked with chlorine, the thrill
of escaping the knotted muscles of my back as sharp
as a knife's edge

(ii)

my mother's weathered skin
folds around her knuckles, pleats of a sun-kissed *sari* in
an after-school memory: her chopping up
purple onions and glistening tomatoes, cupping the slices
in her roughened hands

(iii)

my hair, solid tendrils under sink water,
each scrub of hers matched with my childish
breathlessness, the sun dancing brightly; beside the faucet,
the back of my neck, wet

(iv)

from her digital kisses,
ardent tokens of her unfettered belief in our ability
to outlast the future in a future that stretches so boldly
across time and space that it

(v)

                has already become a memory,
this assimilation of past occurrences; some distant forgetting this
is, my whole life spent narrating my whole life to myself:
a knowing mouth coaxing an amnesiac brain to feel again
that vivid taste of chlorine from

(vi)

              some summers ago,

APHANTASIA

I am aching—a cavity
blown open with resonance,
finding meaning
in its odd mannerisms.

On this side of the nation
I go sky-spotting, bouncing
forward till I greet the beach;
then turn around, because any further
would ruin my shoe-polish.

During the day, I walk past galleries
of awards, but when I elapse
into the evening, I lie in wait
so I may guard a door I can't even
pass through. Who knew in each of us

there is an impenetrable room,
closed off from all corners of this world,
in which knees graze the earth
and a sob can execute its business
in soft privacy.

I would show you what it's like,
concerned as you are—your love reduced
to a blinding squint. I would light a candle
and chaperone you to where I lay,

but there is no air left
for the match to strike. So the temple stays,
kissing the earth in blind faith,
like light and dark decay
in monogamous wait.

DÉBARRASSER

what wouldn't I give to take off this
sticky coat of responsibility—

so covert and so deeply
burned into my skin

what wouldn't I give
to wiggle out of

this cloak-body, a kaleidoscope:
so noisy and so full of mirrors

what wouldn't I give to seat my mind
beside me, a therapy session with myself—

so electric, preventable, and culpable

the sight of my plattered head

PULP

Always the marching band;
always the paper planes,
the demise. Nothing
works any longer, although
the pains remain alleged.

If only truth and
a news report were one
and the same. Wouldn't
I just love to tear up
the whole damn thing.

Instead, I write the words
I despise, I breathe back
the air which brings me spite.
All of us are hungry.
Won't somebody help us?

I wore the corset of winter
for one month of breath.
I even made sure
to wear brick-wall armour,
but the weather here
won't relent.

I've been calling for help
my whole life. I've been writing,
it's been helping, and
you've been reading me.

What a flirt, each of us—
Pulp and word. It is supper
time, and nothing is all right,
again. And that is the best news
I have heard in a while.

INHERITANCE

Stand in

pupillary
disguise,

smile reflux,

rely on
jigsaw jaw.

Oh my
          divine cry.
Allegra.
Fine. Civility
crinkles sheets: repeat

on repeat,
this thrifted,
functional grief.

STAIN

There is a stain on me
which no hot shower
can melt, no ocean
dilute.

In sunlight,
you can see through it,
paper-thin and purple
like a bruise that's stayed on
for far too long.

In shade,
you can see through me—
blue as I am in the shame
of the stain that's
worn me down.

No higher power, no act
of grace, no saving face,
no trick of the light
diminishes the stain

which leaks through
my sleeves, soaks all
my clothes. I sit
bare on the floor
with my head hung low.

There is a stain on me
which persists despite
budget cuts, compromising
circumstances, and
bolstered blame.

I would punish it.
I would scrub it away.
I would give it a name
so I could tell it to go away.

I would wash it down
with bleach—or wine—
I would invite it in
just to get on its good side.

But whatever I call the stain,
in there is me. If I banish it,
I banish me.

BACKTURNED ME

I want to be
more than an animal
happening to itself,

so I break open
my spine like
a fortune cookie,

forget your sleight of hand
for the sight of peace.

I comply with tarot readers,
yet I believe I don't
believe in fate.

I study syntax
with a masculine voice.
Pieces of meaning
huddle close, but I turn
your love away.

Do I forgive you?
Only if you had made
different choices.

Should I forgive you?
Only if you knew
how to listen to
better voices.

Now you sit in a fuss, estranged.
Life cracked you right open
and your lifeline won't return.

She is afraid of you,
and you are afraid of life.

Though you wish
the tree of your life
hadn't been felled,
she is too far down
for you to start
a new sentence.

But a fortune teller did tell me,
centuries ago, the story
of a wandering family.

Their young would read frantically
the shapes of their elders' backs,
so that they would learn
the burdens those backs
have borne. So that the lineage
could learn from itself
before it is born.

Well, I'm getting old
and I haven't done much learning.
Instead, I am the camel
still healing
from a broken back.

But do you think
we might be lucky,
that I might have it in me
to write another sentence
in the name we shared?

Luck—of course—
is a loveless marriage
with a better future.

It only works
if we make it work.

CAUTIONARY TALE

Right now, it's better
to proceed slowly.
Let's not publish
our feelings yet.
Instead let's meditate
on the word *collaborate*.

Is the pretence not more
important than the purity
of the moment?
Give the wrong speech
and years of promise
fall from the precipice,
and our love story becomes
a cautionary tale.

You keep putting me off.
Like ungraded papers,
like emails gone cold,
like groceries gone stale.

But because we still have some air
left in our lungs, let's not be so pressed
to express the change in
seasons.

Eggshells have learned
lessons about breaking
that I want to believe
I won't repeat.

MONEY TALKS

I am told the numbers
don't talk. Still, I play
with them daily. My mind
is childishly wild—it says
there is not enough dirt
on this planet to bury

what hurts us. I am diligent,
too, of the forecast on the news.
How nations line up.
How burned backs curve.

Six dollars a grave—
Wouldn't you spare
that much change
for your grandmother?

Six dollars a grave—
Get it while
the anger's still hot.

Get it before
the cops turn
Your pockets, inside out.

HOT-HEADED

So you fucked it up in a way
you didn't know you could.

So you ran a marathon
with your bloodshot eyes,
looking for the exit sign.

So you got to the middlegame
and wondered if it would be
less costly to resign. But I
wanted to see the fists of your
anger bloom, so I fucked it up
in the way I knew I could.

When you came for my throat,
I ran, until you turned around
and called it a draw.

At least we didn't leave a bloodbath
in the shower, at least we cleaned up
the scene we made.
At least we didn't raze
the gardens of our bad thoughts.

Sometimes I think
we need to burn the exit signs
so it's a fair fight
on the nights
we lose our minds.

GASLIGHTER

They say we are bound to repeat
the cycles we fail to expunge.

You practice your favourite
childhood tricks on me.

A wound-up toy, which made such
a fuss, ended up shattered by your feet.

At first you caught me as I leapt to you, naïve.
Then one winter you began to put me down.

You didn't need any alcohol as you watched me,
knowing you could get your way before I sobered up.

If I dissent, you will distill our history to my
tendencies, to bite the hand that feeds me.

Could you kindly remind me who starves me
all week long? Our love was electric. Somewhere

along the line, the fuse was blown.
Now I draw up plans to leave in the inflammable dark.

The neighbours will ask about the ashy smell,
you will gladly blame the smoke of your ire

on the poor design of my nubile mind. Still, I leave
if it means, one day, I could hear my thoughts again.

Bagszippedquick.

I might soon make it out of the thick smoke.
Clouded rear view. Pouring rain.

No man's an island so I drive around town,
looking for an exit sign.

Your reflection, at the end of every street,
halting all the breath in me.

Your fist is full of matches. Your smirk advises me
of all the bridges you will burn down

if I don't turn right around.

WHAT THE LIVING DO

The old aren't afraid of death.
They are afraid of
what the fear of death
makes the living do.

Unwrap the bones. Cut off the fat.
Slice pineapples and down cranberry
juice. Feed the cat raw food. Unload

the dishwasher. Play the news, sober,
on mute. Wait to cross the street
like you have somewhere to be.
Move closer to the beach. Forgive

him when he cheats. Consider
stand-up but never make the mistake
of getting up on stage. Smell the lipstick that you put on
only for yourself. Be late to work again.
Spill coffee just for the thrill. Make

your heart fall till it's ill. Then gather the pieces
in their own time. When your mom calls?
Listen. When you see her, make up a god
if only so the prayers have somewhere to go.
Go paleo. Let the dishes soak. Set the alarm to repeat.
Crawl into bed, on your knees.
Like a body infected with warmth,
nestle in between grief and relief,
and try to catch some sleep.

MIDDLE CLASS

I am a living being: pulse-bodied.

But from where else does the heart come?

A half-remembered thought appears—

No, just turn away, let the feelings go—

Oh, but they won't leave,
so I may as well grieve
how everything I thought I had in me
flees to a better country, moves to a newer home.
Comes already furnished. Short term rental.

Late-night check in—

and out of your state
of existence: It's only accidental.

Don't hold onto the staircase.
Don't stay up too late.

I'll never make it upstairs.
I'll take this weight to my grave.

The cutlery drawer speaks to me,
and my neighbour laughs. But this joke
is not for me.

Downstairs—the same old beat—repeat on repeat—

Clean up after your timid feet.
It's time to see what
the poets have been writing about.
It's time—

                                    to forget another day.
                                          Don't consider
                              lingering in the corridor.

There's deep laughter there.
I know you wish you could learn how it feels—

                        but when I look, I tend to stare.

Well.

                        I'm always setting the table, but the feast
                                          is never there.
                              I'm always cleaning the glasses
                                    we never bring out, the forks
                                    we've so closely held.

Oh, the markets going to crash, they say—
it'll take years to make the repairs.

I know shame makes you want to glare—

                        But we haven't lost anything that was ours—

                        Nothing was ever really there.

WAYS TO LEAVE

Consider moving up north.
Tie your shoelaces, first right,
then left. Stop at the gas station,
greet the cigarette packs.
Unfold the newspaper, but
don't read. Turn up the heat,
it's going to be a long ride.
Wear a jacket years older
than you. Ask its silk lining
for company. Remember
to call in sick for work. Wear
tan boots, turn your phone off.
Think of maple leaves in a sunny
place. Foster a kitten, bake bread.
Fall sick, trip over your shoelaces.
Practice faith as the runt passes away.
Embrace what needs to go.
Meet me by the porch light
for a cigarette break.
Let's rehearse the word gasoline
till our chapped lips go blue.

SHADES OF SHADOWS

The penumbra of grief is a giggle through a mouth of teeth,
which warns the onlooker of sunlight weaving through ancient trees.
The apology is the darkest part—the admission of a moment
taken away. In shadows you found a love for what still moves.
So what if they took your nation away and gave you a name
which costs too much to change. Your nomadic grit is
a crumpled lease, and little light reaches your ribs anymore.
The women across the street can hear your thoughts, but close
their windows; they have lost interest in your pain,
which they will never understand and so never truly shame.
Even behind curtains, you undress the way a wound opens
and caught off-guard in the thick of healing, whisper:
I wasn't done changing just yet.

LANGUAGE BARRIER

My eyes have a foreign accent in the way they speak to yours.
Can you be everything on the surface tonight?

It has been a while since either of us has felt touched
and I can handle the displeasure of not seeing myself
in the mirror. I thrive in places that need my absence.

I can handle it during the day. At night, the same old news breaks:
The truth is always insufficient, isn't it?

Sing a lullaby to me so I can forget my mind for tonight.
It has been a long evening, and the morning will be dark
as a morgue. We may as well start to settle in.

GRIEVANCE PREPARATIONS

If there is a right way to grieve, I did not keep up with it.

If I came to you with an aching weight,
would you help me bury the green body of my dream,
or would digging up my limits be *ad hoc* resuscitation?

Who are you to sing lullabies to a stillborn?

What in you thinks it can keep planting foot after foot,
orchestrate a stampede on my chest?

Dimensions. Lists of needs. Will fail to wake up in you
the shapes of my feelings.

You don't need poetry now,
only need to know what can be done in this world.

As though poets only watch and reign invisibly.
As though the word is not the first world we see.
As though voices of march have no anapest.
As though refusal isn't a *volta*.

As though opening your mouth, having already decided
to yield nothing to this world,
is only a privilege of the powerful.

CONFESSIONAL

I'm being broken into
like a winter chalet.

I am full of precarious wealth;
if I am unresponsive,
you should know
I am simply frozen behind
the thick amber of faith.

Branches lie tattered, while strangers
with eyes wide as fists keep coming
to see for themselves:
my compelling confessional.

What should I say
after grief leaves the room
in a fit of feeling?

The formal feeling comes—
but the rhyme breaks.

A RELATIVE VISITS

When I ask my mother—who is smart and educated—why she would be married to a lion no-name, she cries once in the evening and it's enough to keep a family of three afloat. But you are 33 and have seen the universe—which only stretched outward—and you were told he did not travel to strange places. You were raised with a different set of parents. He was never in the old home, where he made your lap full of toddlers and left grease on your roughening hands. When the new cooks came, you were already sliced in two. You missed your mother who sat you by the moon and the plants, even though it was a small life with pink bricks. It was easy not to be concerned with the world when it was clearly not concerned with you.

They were loud and there was at least some company for your inversions. One day he bought you a dinner table. It was nice to stand up from the plastic pink *chittai*[1]. You weren't very good with words, but you liked how everything found a way to move. When you left for the sea city you were far from what your mother had been. She had a nose the size of a baby fist, and freckles like black *til*[2] seeds. Flaking. You thought of her back home, aging with the pink bricks. Then your youngest brother called. You took the fall for him. At home, the voices of the boys only got louder. One thunderstorm the sky took our rooftop away. I was so worried for him, in this windowless tin house. He worked in a white suit, with pleats which fell to

---

1   chattai: 'floor mat'
2   *til:* 'sesame' or 'mole'

his thighs just right. He would watch you learn to read, though he was a father who was not able to write. It was shameful, yes, but the city needed far too much.

And we never know where she comes from, though she is always there. She was the one you married because in a city of strangers, she made your fist heart open like a baked potato. We never knew why we were alive; we just knew that we were. One year, all the taps in my street ran out. It was loud—and I can really see it now—the day the sun took your mother's back. Before she woke up from her afternoon nap, you ran to the library for your life. And for the first time in your new, status-less life, you found an ice-cream man. He listened to your fears because you brought him exact change. He was too young when he had moved to the city, so he kept cuffing up his thrifted shorts.

They said there were markets with lines of ice-cream men. You were just as old as 18, when the popsicle stick lost its scaffolding, so you went there often. Under the golden sky, you said you were tired of not being able to read. It wasn't too far off, the richness of each meaning. But how far away you were from the parents, who you had a habit of forgetting at the train station. You found love in being an electrician. And after all those nights when you would crawl home, you would finally notice your beard in a grease-lit puddle. An oval bowl of untouched youth. You sniffed but did not drink. When you heard of women going missing, you knew your daughter would be the master of her dreams. So you raised her in the house that would become your grave.

There is no thrill in epilepsy. That's really why I loved you. You were so young with no fear for fire. We are sitting with bread on the neighbour's *tandoor*[3], waiting for it to fall off. Did we have plastic plates yet? No, I guess not. Right, *nana ji*[4]? Yes, not yet. You saw her clean up after the boys, who were getting better at wearing anger, and it was quite clear she was a fixer. Hadn't your hands had enough? And so quickly? She grew taller; you wished your family owned a mirror so you could show her. Even through your cataract eyes, she began to look like someone who would leave this town behind.

What's so wrong with asbestos, anyways?

I didn't know then. I don't know now. Back then we didn't know. We only saw. We had the sun on our backs, and the children on our feet. We had been walking for so long.
If you're really listening, *meri jaan*[5]—go long.

---

3 *tandoor*: 'clay oven'
4 *nana ji*: 'maternal grandfather' (honorific)
5 *meri jaan*: 'my life'

(& The Miracle After)

TWISTED FATE

Flowers arrive at my bedsheets
like Freudian slips come to my tongue.
Unwanted thorns.

With thoughts growing in me
like tumours, I kiss the small feet
of the life I have left.

All the love I have to give
is gone, as though ships crossing the horizon
arrive at a place I never will.

A person is not
unlike a thing: a rose, a hip, a shore.

Like everything else,
it is here or
it is remembered.

Arrive then, like a memory coming back,
the knife twisting in its delayed agony.

Flowers leave stains on my bedsheets,
like skin that continues to gleam
after being bitten by young love.

THE CASE FOR HIBERNATION

I know you've gained weight, even
though you're refusing to get on the scale.
It seems primal to be wanted, to be known
for your unforgettable shape.

But months into this affair, and you disappear
within your clothes. You are trying
to look away from how you look.

Is it working?

You curl up in your chair, reading
about cold-blooded murders
and flushed-down heartaches.

Maybe it would be more prudent
to let our veins crawl slower;
I read on the internet that
bats swallow whole feelings like
gall and pride; and some bears
find a way to move even in torpor.

Where does the will to sleep come from?
Where does the heart learn to beat,
and is it time to stop?

If you haven't gone
on a walk today,
there might be
a strong case to make
for hibernation.

Outside, hell is freezing over.
Our glory days are not crawling any closer.

But now that we've stocked up the pantry,
if we walk deep into
the closet of soft-pulsed dreams,
we might just make it past this winter.

HAUNTING

In the new world,
my tongue is pink & my name is King
and I need not wear my womanhood
like a flag of surrender.

In the new world,
the riots of what did not pass
do not keep me up at night,
and I have never known
the gut-deep ache
of injustice.

He and I have never known
each other's bodies, pressed close,
bible to the chest,
he does not get to
pray for forgiveness.

I did not give him, unknowingly,
what cannot be given. Fury
is not a verb I live in
in the day to day.

My lover leaves
wet myths on my wanting skin,
and they are the only kind of haunting
this body has known.

NO MORE

Today, I don't want to go on a walk.
I don't want to meet my favourite hedges,
or greet my beloved lightless alleys.

Sometimes, the shadow of what's been
falls on what there is to see.

The grey area deepens. I can sing
for another year, but you are not going to listen
to my confessions of love. This year,
I am weeping for the love
I had expected, and the love
I have to give.

I have been raising parts of myself
before I was ready to be a mother,
telling myself I have little choice
in choosing my calling.

I keep writing love stories
which feature you and me,
but today I want
to put the pen down.

FRESH PAGE

So you thought you would never be here.
Thought you had done a good job convincing
the daytime of your intentions to leave and
the nighttime of your intentions to return.

And in the glow of the midnight city,
you held a borrowed pen, convinced
you could write your way out—one more time.
Two cells down, mercy cried for you,
but you had no breath left

to give her. You came to know
that, for years, sound had masqueraded as voice,
but now the mask had slipped
and everyone around you had noticed.

If you spend your life straddling the border line,
you will lose all depth of your feeling. And each visitor
will recite in you an impassioned ruckus, and you
as the guardian of the electric door, will not know
who to let in and who to let go.

Stripped of all belonging, you will want to save
everything you set your eyes on. Hoarding colours,
stocking silverware, you will sit in the vast mansion
of your mind and will dare not speak a word.

Each syllable I speak confirms the constraints
of how compelling I can make
this jailcell lullaby.

It takes falling to your knees, no grace no peace,
to see the power in your own two feet. Thankful
for your warm pulse, you will plan an escape
from the insufferable sight
of a cry gone unheard.

The mind uses tears for ink, insists
on making a new melody
of the same misery. Don't you worry—
when the page of each breath
has been scrawled over,
your lungs will gladly tear
you a new one.

LITTLE LIVING BEINGS

There is something moving
behind the stove. It might have a tail.
It might have a nose. I haven't seen it
but I know it has
somewhere to go.

I want it gone too, dead or alive.
Last night I heard it squeak
with some semblance of life.

I want to say:
Why did you come here,
don't you know what they do
to beings like you?

You are a freeloader. You're not
one of *us*. But when I think
of your matte-brown eyes,
I don't feel like I own the house.

I feel like a young girl
afraid of a mouse.

I know what it's like
to hide from bright lights.

I know what it's like
to only want to stay inside.

I know what it's like
to crawl for your whole life.

If you could hear how I think,
would you forgive me?

I call my neighbour,
who makes you a box, prepares a piece
of cheese. We will feed you
peanut butter—if you could please
just leave.

I am told, "They are as scared of you
as you are of them." This only
doubles my grief. If I could repel you
towards hope, I would.
We will let you go in a park,
but I know it's freezing out there.
Will you find a moment of peace,
before you die, out there?
I don't feel a sense of victory.
Only shame. I saw the cut on your back,
and still wanted you in a bag.

Now you're on your way to a colder place.
If all goes right, you will not be able
to find your way back.

I hope you know the things that
little living beings have to do
to feel bigger than one another.

CHANGE IN SEASONS

Honey, I know
you can't see
a reason for
such a twisted
destiny.

Money is
hard to come by.
But the beggars
will limp till they go
missing at night.

Worries open
doors to dismal
rooms. Grief is
an unwelcome guest
who masquerades
as pleasure.

Tell me how you would like
to leave, so I can
keep you
from proceeding.

Seeds with the most weight
are stones in the palms of those
who fail to retain passion
for late bloom.

CALL AND RESPONSE

I just wanted a sip
of what you had, some thrifted
glory. Some crisp
of advice to spare.

I have been talking
to the rooms. They ask,
"What will come
of you?" And even the clock,
when it's half past noon,
says, "The kind of shade
which could quench your thirst
comes every other century."

So, your tremors help—they
help keep the time. And we
are learning how to go out too:

We, a meagre team, crawled
to the pink park. Glowing clouds
shadowed our white eyes;

they always have a way
of drifting with dignity,

and there is a song here
that we source from reed.

It needs no language,
but you sing it just the same.
Your vowels glimmer. Every time
you pause, I catch the beat.

PARTING

You should feel well
I am addressing the swell
underneath my feet

I am befriending the bricks
at the end of the street
kissing the horizon parting
iridescent seas

I can never get a hold of you
know this feeling never ends
only leans on your shoulders
and rattles your speech
I came this year early for the feast

but it is never the meat we taste
only the sharpness of the knife
and I am being dulled alive—

BY THE LAUNDROMAT ON SAINTE-CATHERINE STREET

This world rules itself
beyond tears. It is an ego
that dials for the police,

it is a human mind
that has never met
peace. I always see
sharply the ways
I cannot divide you

from me. So, you are
my friend—or my enemy?—
like dirt in a potted plant,
like cigarette ash on
the street. Why this
commotion in my heart,
why this disease?

Don't you and I
also share how we
are losing our minds?

I crave something
so much, I kiss the
idea of anything.

I see your fist
raised at me. How
infertile our
communion can be.

Despite the ruckus
on the street,

nothing you do can
displease me.

I will kiss the crumbs
you leave. I am the maze
of feeling that you
so cheekily weave.

CROSSROADS

The way a fire breaks,
the way a hand rips,

the way a breath leaves,
the way each hand wrinkles,

the way the mountains sing,
the way the injustice stings,

the way a feeling starts,
the way two siblings come apart.

The way the workers bring,
the way the work takes,

the way a poem is made,
the way we cartel the dead,

the way we lose our teeth,
the way our bellies split seams.

The place it aches is listening for you.

Listening is the place where healing will begin.

HUNGER

What spans of time work for you—
Haven't you spent enough on mistakes
that you thought were necessities?

Think about how little it takes to
start making up necessities of our own design.

Just how long will you stare into the dark
and cry little whines for the night?
How long will you set mirrors alight
with your meek appearances?

When will you realize
you have both dark of night
and light of cold summer ice?

I am waiting for you,
after you decide to live towards your self
and learn to head towards rest—
rest as the right sacrifice of time.

You must be ready
to change the ready-made bed,

to walk into new rooms
and make them entirely yours.

Kick at the sheets with your two dirty feet:
you have to break into your casket
and steal
who you want to be
yourself.

My hunger has
woken up.
What does not feed me
can leave.

APPETITE

When the streaks of paper
flow with ink, you will gasp and say
that you did not know the cameras
were running.

You raised an idiot girl.
Then leapt back.
The bitter old woman
still had an appetite.

What makes a girl bitter?
What makes a bitch bite?

In both cases, the shame:
She knows.

But what comes
after a bitch
has had a taste,

after an old woman
has made a vow to life?

For some reason
I always remember
the part that comes next.

The lick of my lips.
The click of your jaw.

SLEEP ON IT

Forever cannot be rushed.
It is like trying to see quicker
than the light of everything.
So then what is darkness
but a blink of life's eye,
and a time to forgive all

those who lied to you
when they didn't know
the truth; it stings and aches,
a misplaced rib or a lover
on a boat, but the whole
horizon is quivering, and the sun-
set doesn't reach me fast
enough.

I am trying to rush
into darkness, but forever
cannot be rushed.

BETTER DAYS

Where we came from, it felt
like there would never be better days.

Now you're married
to the idea of a better you.
Quit smoking so you could send
more gifts to me.

And you thought for years
that no one could love you.
I always knew that wasn't true.

But there are things
we cannot make each other see;
so, I went with you
on walk after walk, catching you
when your mind stumbled
over a bad thought.

Now you lie better than me
and have enough life in you
to look at the calendar.

While I mourn all the days
I spent getting my hopes high,
you walk through forests.
You have found new ground
to blossom from.

The oceans, the continents
are familiar aches to me;
so I keep my distance
from the distance.

You're too far ahead
for me to catch up anytime soon,
but I save every postcard
you send me from your better days—
if only for the hope
of visiting one day.

INISCIENCE

t kind of riddle is this?
time you cheat on me,
t as a sign of your fidelity.

it's clear that evil comes
er spending the night open-eyed,
us in the backs of our minds.
od is shot with the hurt
e places to which
t go.

v, one could say
me good news.

eristic of you,
ned. I was just about
n my paranoia,
ou read my mind.

BREATH WORK

In the end, the breath may be
the last thing to leave. But
are you sure you want to go
without having found the all-knowing one
that every mystic turns for?

I remember when you dusted
off the pain, tossed the tissues
into the bin. You said, "Never
could I again."

And I, a soft pulse of *maybe*,
subdued. Laid down in the middle
of a bustling street.
Silence, the grim reaper, brought
all my conversations to a stilted end.

But, in the silence, something
continues. The motions of a river,
or a haunted tune. Flames
of well-earned rage. A long burn.
Many sticks in my sunset-orange fire.

I lose my voice,
then I lose my eyes.

Then I find a God
who is not an active listener,
who takes too long to reply to prayers,
who appears only to disbelievers.

Still, I am changed,
for you see me when
I am both pulse and fire.

Now I can see past
the hot tears in my eyes,
for I is the spirit which breathes
into the heart of every beat,
"I am more—I am more
than me."

JUSTICE

Justice wears the face of the daughter
you would rather not claim.

Justice comes, two generations late,
hair in slicked-back braids, looking like
a cousin or an aunt who
left for another nation
before you got to learn your own name.

Justice weeps hollow. Coughs up
the heart you never had.
Justice buries the dead thing
which should have lived.

Justice crawls, tired
of the grunt work, of the scrub work,
of the work-from-a-home-that-isn't-yours
work.

Justice is timid. Crosses her legs,
but still manages to make
love untamed.

Careful when you pass your reflections.
You might catch her face in the mirror instead.

Justice weeps till late,
then settles in for a dreamless sleep.

Justice sleeps past all alarms,
but is never too late when-
ever she wakes.

MIRROR IMAGE

You cupped together
a bowl of grapes.

I read from it
the syntax
of all your thoughts
which did not branch
my way.

At night, I wedded myself
to you, in front of
the mirror I had bought
to hold all my vanity.

But my body is
the firstmost accessory:
Why don't I
try wearing it?

A pupil bows,
but its gaze is misplaced.

Sometimes a door closes.

Sometimes I dare
to look your way.

RICHES

This way of leaning in
has startled you—
your heart's so deer-like
that it's halted the tracks of my mind.

Your mother is dead.

And yes, you didn't
have a quarter-life
epiphany—
but all is well.

I did not expect to smile
for traitors to make a living—
but all is well.

I know we are repenting,
for one and the same thing—
the kind of wounds we can only
nurse back
to wealth.

WORK SONG

We had not woken up when we had expected to,
and I knew: the days of trembling
with joy, which was loaned and earned,
were over.

We rose, singing, like our voices came from
somewhere other than our plexus.
Adamant, we wanted each other's limbs
to rest on—some solace in the end-
less days.

We kissed like our first loves
had changed their mind for the better;
like our parents' ashes were
a fistful of pollen, and nothing
more insidious than a rose
could grow inside our ribs.

Deeper and deeper we went,
because our only work was
loving; seeing the barren earth;
and turning the roots up—
your tangled hair bunches and you sigh,
eager to be held
by something bigger
than yourself.

ON RESTRICTIONS

Come on in, they say.
There is no new tomorrow,
but we can try.

Homeless, aching for space,
I buy any air I can share.
But could I exchange
the ground
for a second sky?

I am fed up with rule breakers,
sweet traitors bargaining
for gentler restrictions,
while strict prohibition
smears my face
and meridian divides
taunt my fate.

I watch the ball in the park
passing from hand to hand—
the sweat hardly
a benign mistake,
only a lucky expression
of a would-be embrace.

What kind of truth is it
to say that the starving
are very good at fasting?

The humour of the unspeaking wind
comes to kiss away
the persistent bellyache.

HOW TO FIND GOD

Make peace with a stolen ring.
Call it hope, but know
that scratching the itch underneath it
will be futile.

Say you will sing
on your dying day, then
live out a life of silence.

Keep your gut benign and thin,
like a knife kept out to dry
on a washcloth by the sink.

OPENINGS

The constant entrance of feeling
is the delight—

The aim is to rob me of feeling.

I myself have been the same
self that I had always been.
By my self, the same
self, I have been for so long.

Help me forget the lies and the snide.
The scars at the horizon of my hips,
the curves of my malignant breasts—

Stay. Stay because you are
yourself, so unknowable it is
a pleasure to make you shake.

Wrapped in the delight of summer
lovers, all playful and in the middle
of the courtyard, you might just

make me bite. So much new-ness is in.
Let us unravel each sense,
like imported toffees salvaged
from the dumpsters under our tongues.

It hurts to taste you. How you enter
my senses hurts, but who else do I know?
I let you come in
         like the breath of a life
I could have had if I hadn't stopped
breathing, feeling, being scarred.

Who affirms your truth but you?
Who, when we have gone to hell,
will say how well we lived
but us?

PURPOSE

This is how you do it.
You open the door to the backyard.
Spring air keeps you company
as you put on a new record,
and watches over you as the dust hoarded
beneath your furniture
finally comes to light.
It knows the day started on
the wrong foot—
but that's no reason
we can't make it right.

We lay out the blankets
stained with acrylic paint
and, with a yawn, accept
the somberness, which tickles
the backs of our knees.

But in front of our eyes, we find
new colours to hold up against the sunlight.
Though labour is necessary,
it is not purpose. So when
does labour end
and purpose begin?

Perhaps when we sat beside
each other, chipping at the faded paint.
When you heard the day fly
overhead, and you waved, but said that today
you would rather stay by my side.

Perhaps when I saw your hands scrape
the surface of the old with such vigour
that we uncovered the start of something new.

FREEFALL

Your dreams are costlier than you think. But I am not
in the business of going home anymore.

Heart more thunderclap than mud, don't you
tell me it was not shockingly warm
how mouths carried your name across mahogany rooms.

Sometimes, the corpse is only *quotidien*. It falls onto a floor
of empty mouths—
and the truth sounds not like clatter
but like swallow:

Myself catches me here.

A life saved
          is a life denied.

Sometimes, two hands hold together a face
and the day can burst into sun-streaked flames.

Rob your doubts. It's time
they pay up.

FAITH

My mother is not a writer, yet she speaks like a poet.
She tells me to be a leaf—aloof, a leaf does not
wonder to where it will float.

(I wonder if leaves do wonder,
but I keep my wonder to myself.)

A leaf, she repeats,
sways, is tickled by currents,
sprawls on the water surface,
but never fights what is coming its way.

Suddenly, I am swimming alone,
backstroke, on choked chlorine.

My buoyant body rotating, the laps of water
brushing under the crevices of my back, the day
turning me on the glistening water, beautifully
and emptily. My body a compass
as fruitless as a summer afternoon.

RIOT

Today, I announce my existence.
I decorate myself with the language
of birds, festoon my hair with flowers.
You have taken the life out of me
so I will snatch it back with my pink claws.

So daring is the certainty that the universe
bites its lip; anticipation is a cruel song,
which you bet I'll make you sing with your ribs.

I never came from them, anyway.
Do you see the colours with which I burst?

Their vivifying fury should tell you
what is causing the ruckus down your street:
The silent riot of my existence.

THE ABSENCE OF GUIDANCE MAKES ME SING

You can only take me so far,
but I know I will go further.

And it's your delusion
to think I forgive frivolously.

And yes, I would slap back
but it would only add to the noise.

Why is it only in your absence
that the songbird chirps?

Why is it only in your anger
that I feel like I know you?

I know how long the heart beats,
and I want to age with intention.

I can't keep going this way,
this stain has soaked up enough attention.

I wish I could heal for you;
but I am not the wound,

only the miracle which came after.

Notes

Some poems in this collection have appeared in various literary magazines and journals:

ILLEGIBLE was first published in *Glass: A Journal of Poetry* (April 2022).

A performance of BACKTURNED ME and A RELATIVE VISITS was featured in the Muse Arts Toronto's HAPPENING: Multicultural festival (May 2022).

BY THE LAUNDROMAT ON SAINTE-CATHERINE STREET was first published by *Cathexis Northwest Press* (January 2021).

FREEFALL was first published in *carte blanche* (Issue 39, October 2020).

OPENINGS was first published in *yolk* (Issue 1.1, October 2020).

WORK SONG and PULP were first published in *Déraciné Magazine* (May 2020).

HAUNTING was first published in my poetry chapbook *DREAM FRAGMENTS* by Cactus Press (October 2020).

HUNGER and LANGUAGE BARRIER were first published in *Dream Pop Journal* (Issue 10, Summer/Fall 2020).

DIFFUSING TENSIONS was first published in *Stanza* (April 2019).

* * *

ILLEGIBLE was written when I was doing investigative work in Montreal, Canada as a Local Journalism Initiative (LJI) reporter. I reported for *Parc-Extension News*, writing for the most multi-ethnic and densely populated area in the metropolis. In June 2021, I investigated a COVID-19 outbreak in a manufacturing facility. Nearly all the infected workers came from India, like me, and had left for Canada for better treatment; instead, they were exploited and subjected to unsafe conditions. In ILLEGIBLE I reflect on my shared ancestry with readers of my journalistic work. Specifically, I focused on the grief of the Sikh community and the trauma caused by the 1947 India-Pakistan partition. The wounds involved rioting, blood—trains which arrived laden with corpses. As my grandparents lost their homes during the partition, I carry the wounds. To read about the partition and testimonies of survivors, visit https://exhibits.stanford.edu/1947-partition.

FREEFALL is named after the poem "Free Fall" by Mark Nepo. The concluding lines of CONFESSIONAL are based on the poem "After great pain, a formal feeling comes—" by Emily Dickinson.

Acknowledgements

I remain overwhelmed by the support and sense of community I find in the Montreal literary community, especially as I promoted my poetry chapbook *DREAM FRAGMENTS* by Cactus Press in 2020. In particular, I would like to thank members of the Caesura Poetry Collective, who were a lifeline for me during the pandemic. Willow Loveday Little, Patrick O'Reilly, Jerome Ramcharitar, Samara Garfinkle, Derek Godin, Matthew Rettino, Jacalyn Den Haan, John Withers, Mariana Jiménez, and Laura Chan: Thank you for the support, feedback, and laughter. Thanks too to Patrick O'Reilly and Devon Gallant for comments on an initial draft of this manuscript.

I am also grateful to my mentors and friends in the Montreal area for supporting me through the events which inspired this collection. Rozlyn Henderson and Heather Goad: It is an honour to be in your company.

Many thanks to the team at Guernica, including Michael Mirolla, for seeing the vision behind my debut full-length collection, and Anna van Valkenburg, for making this collection better.

I would not be here without my ancestors. I will never take for granted their labours and their joy. That includes you, Mumma and Papa.

About the Author

Avleen K. Mokha, also known as Mirabel, is an award-winning poet based in Montreal. Originally from Mumbai, India, Mirabel holds a B.A. in English Literature and Linguistics from McGill University. Mirabel was the 2019 winner of McGill's Peterson Memorial Prize for Creative Writing. Mirabel's poems have appeared in *carte blanche*, *Yolk Literary*, *Dream Pop*, *Glass: A Journal of Poetry*, and more. Her writing has been supported by the Quebec Writers' Federation Fresh Pages Initiative for promising writers from underrepresented backgrounds. Mirabel was the spring editorial intern at *Creative Nonfiction* and an editor and literary liaison for *Persephone's Daughters*, an international magazine devoted to survivors of abuse. Mirabel's debut poetry chapbook, *DREAM FRAGMENTS*, was published by Montreal's Cactus Press in Fall 2020; the collection received critical acclaim from *The League of Canadian Poets* and *PRISM International*. She has performed her work across Canada, facilitated creative writing workshops, and curated a range of literary events. She is currently pursuing graduate studies to become a speech-language pathologist. *The Vanishing Act (& The Miracle After)* is her first full-length poetry collection.

MIX
Paper
FSC® C100212

Printed in February 2023
by Gauvin Press,
Gatineau, Québec